Boa Editions
INDEPENDENT PUBLISHING SINCE 1976

PAGAN SKY

Books by Michael Waters

Sinnerman 2023
Caw 2020
The Dean of Discipline 2018
Celestial Joyride 2016
Selected Poems (UK) 2011
Gospel Night 2011
Darling Vulgarity 2006
Parthenopi: New and Selected Poems 2001
Green Ash, Red Maple, Black Gum 1997
Bountiful 1992
The Burden Lifters 1989
Anniversary of the Air 1985
Not Just Any Death 1979
Fish Light 1975

The Bicycle and the Soul: Prose on Poetry 2024

Edited:

Fruits of the Earth: Harvest Poems (with Mihaela Moscaliuc) 2025
Border Lines: Poems of Migration (with Mihaela Moscaliuc) 2020
Reel Verse: Poems About the Movies (with Harold Schechter) 2019
Contemporary American Poetry (with A. Poulin, Jr.) Eighth Edition, 2006
Seventh Edition, 2001
Perfect in Their Art: Poems on Boxing from Homer to Ali (with Robert Hedin) 2003
A. Poulin, Jr. Selected Poems 2001
Dissolve to Island: On the Poetry of John Logan 1984

PAGAN SKY

NEW AND SELECTED POEMS

2000 – 2025

Michael Waters

AMERICAN POETS CONTINUUM SERIES NO. 225

BOA EDITIONS ROCHESTER, NY 2026

Manufactured in the United States of America

First Edition
23 24 25 26 7 6 5 4 3 2 1

Publications by Boa Editions—a nonprofit corporation under section 501 (c) (3) of the United States Internal Revenue Code—are made possible with funds from a variety of sources, including public funds from the Literature Program of the National Endowment for the Arts; the New York State Council on the Arts, a state agency; and the County of Monroe, NY. Private funding sources include the Max and Marian Farash Charitable Foundation; the Mary S. Mulligan Charitable Trust; the Rochester Area Community Foundation; the Ames Amzalak Memorial Trust in memory of Henry Ames, Semon Amzalak, and Dan Amzalak; and contributions from many individuals nationwide. See Colophon on page 131 for special individual acknowledgments.

Cover Design: Sandy Knight
Cover Art: Ronald Sloan
Interior Design and Composition: Isabella Madeira
Boa Logo: Sandy Knight

Boa Editions books are available electronically through BookShare, an online distributor offering Large-Print, Braille, Multimedia Audio Book, and Dyslexic formats, as well as through e-readers that feature text to speech capabilities.

Cataloging-in-Publication Data is available from the Library of Congress.

State of the Arts
NYSCA

Boa Editions
250 North Goodman Street, Suite 306
Rochester, NY 14607
www.boaeditions.org
A. Poulin, Jr., Founder (1938-1996)

CONTENTS

NEW POEMS

SELECTED POEMS 2000 – 2020

for Mihaela

close… then closer—

"Thought he, it's a wicked world in all meridians; I'll die a pagan."
—Ishmael, on Queequeg

"All right, then, I'll *go* to hell"
—Huck Finn

PAGAN SKY

NEW POEMS

LATE PIANO LESSON

On the cobwebbed upright   play desire

Ignore the brittle score   improvise each measure

Find a timbre that calms   your arthritic hand

Play hunger Albert Ayler   instructed his band

Don't play regret   your bedtime ritual

Better to pummel   a brief cacophony

Think Jerry Lee   his piano on fire

Unlearn the psalms   play desire   play desire

CLEAN ASSHOLE POEM

Lucy's girlfriend, after several mojitos,
    Insisted that friendship without sex
        Was the most intimate relationship,
Quoting Chekhov: "If you're afraid of loneliness,
    Don't marry," while sober Lucy wept
        All night on a poolside lounge, but today
Lucy shuffles off the beach & drops her dachshund
    On the condo lawn, twists the spigot handle,
        Then lifts the dog's tail to hose his asshole,
A goofy grin on the dog's face as cold water
    Toggles his anus while Lucy's forefinger & thumb
        Tug clumps of shit clinging to his rump &
I'll skip this evening's community potluck, but recall
    Peter Orlovsky, holy Beat madman poet
        Who wrote *Clean Asshole Poems*:
"I get to work naked… / & quite a few times / the sun
    Gave me a warm kiss / on the center of my ass hole /
        Wile bending deep down doing some funney work,"
Who married Allen Ginsberg in '55,
    Who jerked off at Frank O'Hara's funeral in '66
        In homage to the erotic   charge of poetry
& now Lucy & her dachshund with his clean asshole
    Parade past, the hose limp in wet grass,
        O Lucy, all that we do so willingly for love.

TRIVIA NIGHT AT KIKI'S BEACH BAR

Las Terrenas
Dominican Republic

Names pixelate the outdoor screen
Like newly minted winter constellations
Before trending toward erasure:
                                        Mr. Bean,
Dallas, Ding Dongs, Electric Slide, Brown
V. Board of Education…
Every ten minutes an obscene parrot's
Shrugged shoulder to shoulder. Whomever
That bird shits upon
                              must buy the house a round.
The stench of glittering stalls
Where fishermen gut dorado, the starry canon
Reflected beyond the barren reef…
Huckleberry Hound. Parcheesi. *The Hobbit*.
I harbor a single question:
                                   who wrote the Book of Love?
Sappho. Shakespeare. Erica Jong. Lorena Gallo.
Regulars know   her married name as Bobbitt.

MISERICORD

the mercy seat—a ledge under a hinged seat to allow monks to rest during services, often depicting sexual imagery

Those nights I watch you dream—
Grimacing like the gargoyle, grinning
Like the taken-from-behind mistress
Carved in relief on the nether side of seats
In choir stalls of cathedrals—
I know you're flying, looking down
As your breath quickens, face furrows.
You're clocking the two of us, bound
Like hounds stuck together
In a copulatory knot &
Blaspheming the airy architecture,
Before you rage once more back into your body
To resume the earthiness of our marriage.

PAGAN SKY

Las Terrenas
Dominican Republic
2020

Our pandemic proved a pleasure
Granted by the hands-off gods
Who loom above the island

We'd been told to leave, those avuncular
Gods who indulge adolescent
Rebellion, so we stayed

To stroll miles along the strand
Seeing no one, to lie together,
The landscape Edenic & eerie,

The setting of an apocalyptic movie,
While the less affectionate gods
Let their rancor sour cities, doom the old.

Truth be told, we rode out the pandemic
Barefoot & barefaced through distant
Cries & crises beyond our horizon

Where the sun still rose each day
Until we shone like the first
Two people on the planet, not yet

Guilt-ridden, unashamed
    To be naked & alive
        Below all the hooting gods.

SPOUSAL SONNET

How kind we are to each other, mostly.

You Windex, I chamois, we Pledge. We couch.
We've chilled white Bordeaux— you slip raspberries
Into each glass, or ripe slices of peach.
We sushi, we Hulu, doze knee to knee.

You tuck billets-doux among toiletries
Packed for my overseas flight. I mail cheese,
Dark chocolates to complement merlot
You sip most nights before sleeping alone.

Once home we Pantene, Dove each other's skin.
We whisper, slipper, spin Keith Jarrett low.
"I love you," I say. "Love you," you echo…
"As much as I'm able to love anyone."

How kind we are to each other, mostly.

PEDESTRIAN MALL

Loud obscenities reverberated in the dim
Storefront recess, two tongues lashing
As my wife & I strolled near dusk
Past the shuttered Sunglass Hut.

Someone wept, so I trespassed shadows
Until the couple grew visible,
Her back pressed against the display window.
Are you okay?
                    Are you okay? echoed weakly.

The guy hulked toward me &— O jeez—
I recognized my humdrum colleague.
Michael, he mumbled, *just talking...*
As his wife gazed into her shoes.

I turned to leave but was struck by my wife
Standing alone, squinting in,
Still touched by the slanting sun. Didn't I
Belong with this couple in the reflective

Darkness, each of us momentarily
Ashamed of who we had become?
When I emerged to grasp her hand,
I was no longer her faithful husband.

AFTER THE ARGUMENT

And once, although I wasn't here,
you left three roses on my stair
—John Logan

And once, our bed October cold, the furnace not yet
Startled, the soft enwombing flannel sheets
Still mothballed in the cedar chest, you

Turned to me in a whisper of warmth, not quite asleep,
Murmuring about the girl with chartreuse hair
Who left three roses for the raconteur

Who wanted to be her lover, so what could I do
In my threadbare sorrow but burrow
Close to you, then closer—

PARABLE

That Mary Magdalene washed the feet of Christ
Remains a lesson in humility that lies

Beyond me, though I kneel in the vestibule
To wipe each paw with a worn dishtowel

As our dog practices patience, knowing
Leftovers will soon brim her bowl,

Cold tapwater slosh from its steel twin.
She allows me to tug clumps of snow

That cling like burrs to her belly skin.
Having shouldered the storm, we comfort within.

Our dog is as old in dog years, love, as we are.
Does it matter that we've hurt each other

Among the million moments that make a life,
That we've not gentled feet with tears and hair,

That Magdalene is known both as a whore
And, as scholars claim, Jesus' wife?

MAGDALENE

Donatello, 1453

The wood seems to weep,
White poplar still alive.
Flowing hair ropes the ragged
Shift at the waist and torn strips
Swathe scabbed thighs.
She lifts hands toward prayer,
Though palms never touch.
Cavernous eyes and parched lips
Express anguish—
Having witnessed her man
Step from the gaping tomb
Only to evanesce, herself left behind,
She knows her faith need no longer
Deepen, but like her flesh
Must petrify. You and I
Waver before this six-foot-two
Statue, ignored by the sinner
To whom we don't matter.
Her gaze is not upward but beyond,
And if we turn we might glimpse
The world that will still exist
When one of us is gone.

for Mihaela

FIRST DEATH

I noticed them as we arrived, more shade than shape,
More slash of ink than breast or beak
Among branches outside the funeral home, those crows
That morphed into the unknown
Mourners who viewed my cousin, OD'd teen.
No one knew them. A darkling dozen,
Sleek in sheens of black gabardine,
Wingtips buffed to an ungodly shine,
They hunched together in a dim recess,
Never inching closer to the coffin
Or offering condolences before slipping away,
All the aunts unsettled, the guestbook unsigned.
Falling asleep on my father's shoulder,
I may have dreamt this curious company.
I looked for them later in the lot, but they were gone,
Calligraphy turned cypher, I think now that I'm older,
Though as a boy I stared for hours into the barren trees.

BROOKLYN LIMBO

I begged my mother to watch as I raced
The corridor toward the tenement's exit,
Bare bulbs long burnt out.
I tore past the darkest square, the recess
Where devils and demons conspire
To drag sinners down cellar stairs.
I'd seen depictions in my catechism,
Horned and hooved and hairy creatures
Grinning as they grasp each child's ear.
The cellar was not flush with fire,
But rank with sulfurous sewage water
And slick with centipedes and mold,
A grave from which I'd never be called.
When I looked back, the door was closed.

APATITE

—a mineral ground for pigment in the early
Qing Dynasty, component of bones & teeth

If I split this oval stone in two,
I might unlock some long extinct
Bird feather shade of blue.
I lie on my back, grass
Cold & sharp against my scruff.
Above me streak the Geminids,
Chalk strokes on black infinity.
I squeeze the stone to stop myself
From falling into mystery,
Then slip that gloss inside my mouth
To tongue its primal circuitry.
Apatite sparks each cell in my body.
When I enter the earth, candle
Rendered to waxy puddle,
My teeth will splinter
Into mosaic glitter,
Mineral blue, apatite
To seethe against the night.

PALMISTRY

In this hour before your death, you awaken,
Then shower, swivel as lather
Swirls clockwise down the drain.
You buff your body with a plush tan towel.
In this hour before your death, you step
Onto the scale to take pleasure in pounds
Lost last summer. You preen
Before the steam-fogged mirror.
On this ordinary Monday, you hum some 90s
Tune, *Linger,* or *Nothing Compares 2 U.*
Both conjure more than one ex-lover,
But in this decade your life is simple.
You prop the blue toothbrush
Next to the crumpled tube of Crest
In the painted ceramic souvenir cup.
Downstairs, your spouse brews coffee.
In this hour before your death,
Your mouth's all minty, so fresh
That you exhale into your palm,
Where the life line joins the fate line,
To smell the sweet success of your breath.

MOUNT HOPE CEMETERY

Lambertville, NJ

We form a line in cold rain
Until it is my turn
To grasp the shovel, left hand

On the shaft, right on the handle
To heft a small heap of dirt
From the graveside pile,

But I skip the shovel, wanting
To feel soil, its cool,
Granular texture, &

Summon for a moment
His kindness & tics & humor &
Affection for small mammals,

Summon the single, unadorned
Room where he endured
Slow diminishment,

Then let the dirt seep
From my fist onto the oaken urn
Within which the gray chalks

Of American poet Gerald Stern
Settle into their deep, abiding
Discipline.

1925-2022

GWENDOLYN BROOKS

1917-2000

On April 21, 2012, the United State Postal Service issued a 45¢ First-Class Forever Stamp to honor the poet.

I dreaded the rush after Sunday Mass
As I dumped the dozens, feathers & shit
Still stuck to shells, into a metal vat,

Tripped the mixer, then strained the mess
And splashed the scrambled onto the griddle.
I cleaned the coffee machine the size of a droid

While sweat rilled beneath my paper hat
To wet the net bridling my beard.
My bile shames me now. Someone else

Works those early morning shifts, someone
Still wearing her Pancake Shack smock
While waiting in line at the post office

For money orders to pay overdue bills, who
Paperclipped exact amounts of dollars, but
Lost track counting coins, who asks me,

Shifting behind her, for fifteen cents
To make up the difference for one last stamp,
Then passes three nickels to the impatient clerk

For the perforated portrait of Gwendolyn Brooks
Who would have hugged this woman hard
And split with her a single egg for breakfast.

OTHERWORLD

Our dozen or so ringed the holy well,
Some stooping low to cup in palms
Cold water seeping through stone.
This being Ireland, two swans
Frothed the estuary. Someone twined
Her mauve scrunchie onto a branch
Among pandemic masks & strips of scarves,
Ragged decoration in raucous devotion.
Lapsed, I stood my ground among believers
Who gathered stones for cairns, who
Blessed themselves more than once
With soppy fingers as the whole country
Greened around us & lines of poems
By Kavanaugh, Heaney, & Boland
Wound through sky briefly bluing.
I listened closely to the wind-thrust words.
We tromped through mud back to the bus
Idling in mist of its own making,
Then raced the weak light west as rain
Shawled our surfacing reflections.
Our faces wept beside us as we slept.

ASHKENAZI BIRTHMARK

Maybe the parapsychologists are right
To claim that birthmarks
Intimate wounds sustained in prior lives,

An idea darker & more complex than believing
The heart-shaped stain on your daughter's back
Resulted from a mother's love of strawberries.

This perfectly round benign brown button
Sewn onto my forehead in the womb
Must speak of a maternal great-uncle

Executed in Vinnytsia, 1942,
The bullet hole from which a plume of smoke
Escaped like a soul, if one believes in souls...

That whole side of the family gone now,
No one to ask about the ancestor
Named Alexei or Grigory or Ze'ev

Whose corpse bore a bullet hole on his brow,
This birthmark through which the unhoused wisp
Spirals into cursive to strike this page.

VISITATION

Dorothy Waters
1927-2022

No visitors. Covid. I haven't seen my mother in months,
But stand now on a grassy hump
Outside the locked-down memory care facility
Where she's been propped in the window of her room,
Grotesquely lipsticked, thinning hair
Unbrushed, askew. I wave. How we adapt.
August dusk—the reddening sky my backdrop.
And what does my mother see? Her reflection, then me,
The son she bore seventy years ago,
As we merge once more.
Shimmering in glass, I'm within her, without.
I smile, not wanting to startle, to shout,
But it's the double whammy of her skull
With its horrible rictus grin
Peering through translucent skin
That's staring back at her, wanting in.

THE AFTERLIFE

When my mother died, I missed my father
Thirty years dead but somehow still
More corporeal
Than the shrunken woman
Who gibbered in tongues
Like some desert-addled saint,
Her glossolalia less spiritual
Than dementia's failure
To prevent her from airing
Never-ending complaints.
Before his death, my father
Learned to shut his ears
As her babble began to rise
Decibel by decibel
Into a CIA black site's
Pummel of death metal.
He even struck a deal
With God:
If he stayed his palm, if
He pretended to listen
To her vexed desires,
He would evade
A second hell, never
Be forced to feed
His fingers one by one
To those inexhaustible fires.

BROOKLYN SHOWDOWN

That mean motherfucker on one side of the fence,
Black bullet nose thrust through diamonds of mesh
As I barked back, both of us feigning outrage
Along the junkyard rim until the wire ran out,
The gate open, nothing now between us
But the Bed-Stuy heat...
                                                & he who'd dozed all night,
Unchained, on gravel & glass, pulled up, loped off,
Our morning routine accomplished, identities intact,
That mongrel still the most crazed cur on the block,
While I strode toward the concrete park
Where friends idled, ready to rip each other apart.

TO A THIEF WHO DIED YOUNG

You stole underwear from Kohl's & Target
By pinching thongs from bins, faking a sneeze,
Then blowing your nose in those clumped panties
Before stuffing them into your pocket.
No e-tags back then to whistle metal.
If you wanted something small, you took it:
Cassette tape, Hershey's bar, those minty trees
To freshen the air in your slept-in car,
All slipped down the back of black jeans.
You bristled with 90s Spice Girls power
Each minor theft conferred. You greened your hair.
Nabbed & fined, you crowed the misdemeanor,
A street kid's diploma, your MFA
In a craft more reckless than poetry.

THE POISONING

for Mairéad

Lesions blot your body,
Shallow red concavities
Like postholes mapping skin.

Nerves wired to your spine
Detonate without warning.
You'd pried panels off walls

Of the forsaken family pub,
Hauled out debris, wanting
To return to your ancestral village

Some vestige of community,
And drew into your lungs
The loosened arsenic dust

As Ireland greened around you.
Amateur carpenter daughter
Spackling drywall, cutting trim,

Black wheelbarrow brimming
With tainted slats of pine,
You must have sensed the barbed

Particles of the past in your throat,
The tumultuous chronicle
Of that riven country.

The toxins will weaken with time,
    The blisters fade from your face.
        Now you're a citizen of history.

GETHSEMANE

Late night in the guest room, between our hosts'
Bedroom & the nursery where their toddler
Calls & calls, we lie awake, struggling to trust

This new parenting, never taking the child
Into bed, not soothing her when she wails,
Allowing her to exhaust herself toward sleep.

That cry rose across fields at Antietam,
Those wounded boys so far from home,
One voice triggering another, *mama!*

Like a series of muffled explosions
Echoing into the future where I hear
Tyre Nichols & all our dying citizens

Keening from the crib, their weak bleating
Unanswered though never-ending, our country
Awake or maybe sleeping, as we are not.

DIRT DEVIL

That first year all I could do
Was gentle the yowling bundle
Bassinet to bed, then lie awake
While my wife nursed & gazed
Into the baby's eyes, that primal
Bonding. Daytimes I'd rock
Our haywire alarm clock
Until my wife soothed her,
One breast then the other,
As I stood stubbled,
Woozy & dry-nippled,

Distant until
The hour our toddler flipped
The switch on the idle
Devil which hissed alive
& didn't she leap cat-like
To clamp arms around my neck,
This daughter so small
You'd have thought me
Hugging myself, a flawed man,
An oddball, but never
This spellbound father.

for Kiernan

REPORT FROM OCTOBER

Ocean, NJ / Kyiv / Gaza

Wind loosens the squirrely last leaves.
Plump jack-o'-lanterns glow

Doorstep by doorstep as the street
Seems to lengthen & narrow,

A gauntlet of goblins.
Almost Halloween. That time of year

When whatever you wear is wrong.
Furnace off. Furnace on.

Cobwebs drape low branches.
Twix & Kit Kats mix in baskets by the door.

All the children will be ghosts & zombies,
Spattered with blood.

They'll stagger among the luminaries
Like children in war.

That time of year. Horror near, horror far.

NATURAL HABITAT

No photo, no other sightings, not even scat.
Then a dead fawn, partly eaten, mostly hidden—
That Sunday's 5K postponed as rangers
Combed the park. Nothing. Minor mystery.
Neighbors resumed routine activities.

Then we spotted the creature, not sure
At first—mountain lion, maybe coyote?— rippling
Among trees, tan, beige, sunset copper,
A reddish shade when sunlight caught her, &
What a stunning beast

We must have seemed, running abreast,
The long spine of us, our unnatural colors:
Magenta, pink, some otherworldly blue.
We had our proof. The world made sense,
Though the creature, not seen again,

Carried off with her
The confusion of the new, nylon or polyester
Like water over skin, or skin over water,
Highlighter green or metallic silver
Meaning prey, or maybe predator.

HUMAN DANCE

Heteropoda venatoria
Las Terrenas, DR

Like a lopped off hand exhumed,
Flexing once more in night air,
So large the calico leaps onto a table,
The spider stops time with its sudden arrival,

Drawn by porch glare or bowl of kibble or
Mob of moths.
                    Who can tell what beckons
A creature with eight eyes, two fangs,
An abdomen fat as a blown bubble...

I perform the moves we bust
When we greet the many-legged,
A mash-up of cartoon contortions
Until one Croc finds its mark,

My limbs still spasming like the struck
Spider's.
          Vertical animal,
I assume my spot
Among all the alien breathers.

SELECTED POEMS 2000 – 2020

BROOKLYN WALK-UP

Too often my mother told the story
Of bundling me into the red snowsuit,
Leaving me scarved & ear-flapped,
Zippered to the chin, baby-bootied
Upon the quilted bed
While she wrestled the carriage
Six flights down tenement steps
Only to return to a locked door,
The key nestled in the handbag
Dangling from the inside hook.
A cry like no other rose inside her.
She rushed again down crooked stairs
Out onto Covert Street,
Past the deli & funeral parlor,
All the way around the corner
To the Irving Avenue alley
Where she grasped then climbed—
This new mother—
The fire escape ladder
Rung by icy rung
To reach the first metal landing, then
Clanged upward floor by floor until,
Crouched upon the uppermost grate,
She could see the swollen,
Immobile, doll-shaped pile.
She raised the unclasped window,
Gathered me, grabbed her bag, descended
Once more the six floors to the cold carriage,
Then raced to the Dekalb Avenue BMT

To meet my father home from work.
Wheeled madly, I slept like a bobbing cork.
She never told him how she'd shut me in,
How she'd gazed through glass
At the clump of cloth,
The breathing heap of wool & cotton
For which she'd leapt beyond her measure.
Motherhood had turned uncommon.
Years later she took such pleasure
In repeating the story, that boy
Swathed like an Andean child
Sacrificed on the mountain peak,
Mummified by the dry, glacial winds,
Never to name his executioner,
That boy her favorite version of me.

AVIAN ELEGY

Then my mother grew smaller,
The length of a wooden clothespin.

Wrapped in tissue,
She lay upon the birdcage floor,
Surrounded by seeds.

Someone had stolen the birdbath from our yard,
Wrested the concrete basin from its pillar,
The pillar from the kingdom of earthworms.

My mother had nowhere to go.
No rainwater to slake her thirst, to absolve her.
I wore her feathered cloche, surrendered
To the silence stunning the trees.

I'm turning the mirror, Mother,
I'm turning the mirror
Off.

SHARK RIVER BRIDGE

That spot in the center of the bridge
Where the seam splits metal, where
The two leaves of the span part
For tuna boats—their 7' rods
Rigged high as though trolling for God—
That spot above the gray waters of the inlet
Where Avon-by-the-Sea arcs into Belmar—
That's where I'll jump some wintry predawn
Once dementia has commenced, before it seeps
Deeper into my brain & swerves me
From my purpose, protects me from self-harm,
Makes my death dependent
Upon those whose love will stay their hand.
I'll wear my black woolen overcoat, its pockets
Jangling with silverware, & wash down
With a tumblerful of vodka
The long-amassed tablets of Ambien
Before leaping toward oblivion.
Watching our elders deepen into dementia,
We rehearse escapes, our exit fantasies.
I will not gaze like my mother beyond the son
Who visits the memory care facility, will not
Pluck incessantly a ghost-hair off my tongue
Or spin & spin again the buttons of my cardigan
Only to focus suddenly on his face & whisper—
Those glinting hooks descending— "I want to kill you."
No. I will not.   I've picked my spot.

PRAYER WITH CARAVAGGIO

I will no longer enter a cathedral
Unless it conceals a single
Caravaggio
In a recess reeking of incense
Where one bulb illuminates the oils
That they may shine more darkly,
That I might recognize the human
Flaws in divine depictions
& weep with wonder.
I'd rather stroll the local mall,
The galleria in Milan
Where women burdened with bags
Stop to scratch with one foot
The bull's huge balls for luck.
That mosaic on the tiled floor
Snorts near sliding-open doors
Where summer's dense, ungodly heat
Hammers the falsely frigid air,
While prayers exhaled for centuries
From nearby pews in candled naves
Diminish in the vaulting.
Here is my prayer, murmured over ice
Shaved into a paper cup
Euro'd from a vendor
At the bottom of these cathedral
Steps where I sprawl, syrup
Sweetening my tongue.
I will no longer enter a cathedral,
But wherever I go

I’ll still pray with the sinful
Devotion of Caravaggio
Who paid his prostitute, robed in blue,
To pose for a tableau
As the poxed yet holy
Virgin Mary.

SELF-PORTRAIT WITH DOLL (1920-21)

I have come to hate myself
As Kokoschka despised his doll,
Life-sized, red-haired, perfect in every part,
Horsehair and feathers
Sewn into the image of Alma Mahler
Who'd left him during the war,
But with whom he now slept
As she mouthed in dreams
His scars, gunshot and bayonet,
Until one night in drunken stupor
He forced himself to murder
His mute, immobile lover.
His fantasy was flawed,
And I have come to hate myself
For loving you so imperfectly, for craving
Your body, its clefts and moist creases,
Perfumes and spices,
And all the positions your limbs assume
During lovemaking.
                                        I apologize
For this inexhaustible desire
For your lashes and lobes, the vertical
Slash of your navel,
The light strobing in the hollow
At the base of your spine...
And for your breath, always your breath
Which keeps us both alive.

GOOD RIDDANCE CHICKEN

My wife still cooks some meals
Using my ex-girlfriend's recipes,
Their familiar cursive once thrilling
In those years of exchanging letters
With their catalogs of arousal, divulging
Where we would taste each other
On those weekends we managed to erase
The distance between her home and mine.
Maryland-Connecticut. I-95. Driving
Through downpour or snow, blasting
Cranberries or Counting Crows.
She prepared exquisite meals,
Artichoke Heart Soufflé or
Bass Fillets Poached with Fennel
For my midnight arrival,
Coddled eggs with shallots
For breakfast, then mailed the recipes
So that I might in her absence recreate
Each savory morsel.
                                        Now my wife
Revises each directive, shunning
Grapes but adding orange wheels
Or switching shiitake for wild chanterelle,
Purring with Rihanna on the radio,
Crossing out the name of each dish
At the top of the creased index card
To substitute one of her own invention,
But growing quiet when she reads, again,
Looped at the bottom of her favorite recipe,

The one for Chilled Roquefort Chicken,
"Always better when you add my company."

RED-BILLED FIREFINCH

Lagonosticta senegala

Birds called pithis, sold… across Senegal for a dime…
are believed to carry away sins when set free.
—*The New York Times*

I whisper sins into empty birds,
Then set them free. So many sins, pithis
Untold. I watch them wing the sins away.

I buy finches from vendors in makeshift stalls,
Exotics in cages like sins in souls,
Touch lips to plumage where ears must be,

Then flick my finger to let each bird loose.
Have you seen my sins, scarlet flocks wheeling,
Unbound from my body? Have you witnessed

Modest comets arcing trees, feathery
Fireballs of forgiveness, plump pithis
Looping back now to hook claws within me?

ASHES

Maybe you'll ask our son to scatter
A few ounces of your ashes
Near the Ukrainian border
Where the body of the unknown saint
Unearthed by monks hunting mushrooms
Almost two centuries ago
Refuses to shed its fragrant flesh
Which assumes the spongy
Texture of tallow.
A young girl hiking countryside
During the communist regime,
You cradled the obscene head
And kissed those yellow lips,
Then ate a meal of soup and bread
Hunched alone at a rough-hewn table.
Despite that gesture of devotion,
The monastery will never claim
Fragments of your female frame.
Some believers have wealth enough
To satellite ashes into space,
Nearer My God to Thee,
Though that would be a waste of money.
One ambitious entrepreneur
Presses ashes into CDs
Which preserve the voice of the deceased,
So you could leave a farewell sound
Ghosting within
That round & impossibly thin

Unfashionable mausoleum.

Or

You might task our son with travel
To sow your ashes among the snowdrops
(Snowdrops always your favorite flower)
Lighting cemeteries near your home
Not far from the Ukrainian border.

for Mihaela

GOOD DEAD PERSON

Please don't inscribe my name on a tombstone,
Or place there a passage from my favorite book.
I have no favorite book.

Please don't chisel dates on my...
Please don't buy me a tombstone.

Please don't plant flowers on my grave.
I have no favorite flower.
I have allergies.

Please don't visit when the leaves redden,
Or snow whirls, or crocuses lift their purple cups.

Please don't circle the date on the calendar
To mark the anniversary of my death.
Don't say, "Six years gone," or "Twelve years gone."

When our children mention my name,
Insist that you don't remember me.

Tell them you remember nothing but my love,
Always there like the moon
Over Malta, Romania, the Dominican Republic.

NOBODY'S POEM

In the solitude of this cottage room
Where the only sound is the on-again
Sotto voce whisper of the furnace
And the pipes' insistent knocking
As if the unwanted babe of the Muse,
Mewling creature swaddled in newspaper,
Has been dumped once more on the doorstep,
The floor-to-ceiling bookcase hoarding one wall
Filled with forty-year-old literary journals
Holds its breath.
                                        If I move, if the air stirs,
The dust spouts again the words of poets
Listed in ten thousand Tables of Contents.
Even the journal in which this poem appears
Will be wedged in a wall among its brethren
Until someone down the decades draws it down
To drag one finger down the list of contributors:
Nobody, nobody, nobody, name, nobody, nobody
All the way down to the cold damp ground.

IEŞIRE →

Romania

I keep thinking the meaning of the word
Must be *desire*, so want to follow its arrow
To wherever it's pointing, that ballroom
Through which desire throbs like a wound,
Like the strings of the bass of Charles Mingus.
That's the wherever where I'd like to be,
At the groin's chernobyling epicenter,
On longing's narrow precarious lip,
On the viscous, pearlescent tip of desire.

But the meaning of the word is *Exit*,
Meaning, therefore, *death*, that space I'd rather
Avoid,
          an absence, abyss, an abscess
Raw as a screech chalking a blackboard
Or, louder and rippling outward,
Zero's ceaseless, starless, staticky buzz,
Unlike the seizure-inducing strobe
I keep pretending desire is.

CLASSIC COCKTAIL

Moonlighting as bartender, my father
Bungled home with lipstick on his collar,
Having steadied one tipsy regular
On stiletto heels to her Impala.

No surprise he deflected Mother's glare.
It wasn't the first time he'd come home kissed.
He balled the telltale Van Heusen, then missed
The jump shot into the wicker hamper.

Dad taught me how to mix a martini:
Swirl vermouth in the shaker, snap it fast.
Over cracked ice, pour four fingers of gin.
Stir then strain into the chilled cocktail glass.

Add one pimentoed and toothpicked olive.
Sip until the divorce papers are served.

PERFORMANCE ARTIST

By 1993, AIDS had become the leading cause of death among persons 25 to 44 years old...

late '80s

Our host tapped his demitasse spoon on the rim of the wineglass
Until chime-fall needled the room
And our murmuration ceased,
Then announced that following the armagnac
He would stage a solo masquerade
On the patio overlooking the garden
Ruined, this summer—he could hardly bear it—
By roses sickened with invisible worms.
So we gathered below the evening's demarcations,
Shadows sweeping the vast lawn toward trees
Which, in memory, seem inexhaustible repositories
Of unspoken grief, and waited, feigning patience,
For the performance to commence.
Theatrically,
He shrugged off impending darkness to step before us,
Cobwebbed in a tattered wedding dress,
Pale splotches of russet staining the yellowed silk
Cinching his narrow torso and hips,
Brittle lace crumpled like used tissue,
And the torn train, a shriveled petal, dragging behind him.
Tarnished pearl buttons wobbled on loose thread.
The veil enmeshed each feature of his face,
Blurring nose and chin, erasing eyes,
So he might have been any one of us, though
Red-slashed lips, opened

In the imperfect oval of a scream,
Flashed fiery enough to burn through tulle.
Then he floated in slow motion down stone steps,
Easing onto the grass and out across the lawn,
Pirouetting, in slow motion, toward those trees
In a choreography hurtful in its austerity,
The dress hissing softly behind him,
And some among us began sobbing,
And some among us held each other
Against affliction as the figure grew smaller,
Ghostly beyond the skeletal trellises,
Our host a single wick of flame
Flickering as it crossed the woods' threshold
Before disappearing,
                                        extinguished,
                                                            pfft....

ONE CAW

Against the snow they're silhouettes,
These crows, how many hundreds
Burdening branches, these
Blunt-scissors-&-construction-paper
Kindergarten cut-outs, these
Rorschach blots, sloppy calligraphy,
Or jagged wounds, the sky torn,
But not political, if that's possible.
Then a blast scatters the murder
& any direction they flee is wrong.
Smoke on the hillside. The soldier
Stares, rifle tensed on one shoulder.
He's looking me over, wondering who I am.
I've seen this scene in films, Russian novels,
Old Master oils, Pathé newsreels.
Or on CNN—smoke in the city,
Schoolchildren scattered among rubble—
If that's possible—or blue sky, shade trees,
Suburban sprawl. The police car stops.
The boy stares. How many hundreds.
One caw, then silence.
Something horrible about to happen.

KARAKUL

Romania
2015

In summer the storks nest on telephone poles.
Their fledglings peep over the round rims of straw,
And sometimes spill to the blacktop below
Where feral cats make quick work of their bones.
The nests remain empty all winter, until
Those storks return to the same nests once more.
This winter ISIS has been all over the news,
Dragging blades across journalists' throats,
Kindling gas-soaked soldiers in cages,
Flinging gay students off rooftops of mosques.
Hammering to rubble the ancient sites—
Better to begin again with cruelty
So the world might be purged of its past.
Here as in many parts of the East
Every man of a certain age
Wears a wool karakul through winter.
The best hats are sewn from the pelts
Of lamb fetuses slit from the womb,
And bought by politicians to flaunt and wave
As they march in national holiday parades.
Next in quality are the pelts of newborns
Killed as they slip from mother to pasture.
A single skin equals a single hat.
It's the workmanship and the material,
The wooden needle looping infinities
As the bobbin spins out the fur,

Its incomparably soft liquid texture
With subtle shadings ranging
From eggshell white to northern night
That set the karakul apart, but still
In the back of my mind there endure
The crinkled corpses, the mothers
Crying out for their offspring, and the men
Who continue to perfect their art.

POETRY

—filches dreams from birds,
Pigeons with twisted grins or crooked feet,
Their thumb-thick heads tucked under wings
On cornices overlooking traffic
That throbs and sparks along the avenue
And shivers vibrations up building walls.
These birds drowse despite fumes and noise—
Never vexed by money, or sex,
Or how thoughts wane in lazy minds.
They don't rise in the night to pencil words,
But remain hunched on narrow ledges
Sighing bird sounds—coos and trills—
Which are translated without knowledge
Of avian language by insomniacs
Whose brains hiss with fire as they scrawl
Gnomic verse in the blunt circle of light
Thrown down on the desk near the window.
A flash below... a flax seed beckoning...
This is where poetry originates
Some nights, swiping the reveries of birds
Who quit their perch as morning commences
To scavenge the bus stop for croissant flakes
Fallen from plump lips of dazed commuters.
One finds a button. Another plucks up
A keychain bead—nothing to be eaten,
But how chic it speaks in the busted beak.

MADRIGAL

—the origin of the word is uncertain, probably from the Latin matricalis, *literally "of the womb"*

Eyelash, tongue tip, finger whorl.
Scrotum. A skull
Shifting from archipelago to minor
Continent.
                    Buoyant contentment.
How I wish I could remember
Such leisurely becoming, that
Slow sprawl toward finale,
And recognize once more,
Before death, the barely
Audible madrigal,
That almost visceral,
Unself-conscious whistling
That summoned me,
Little god roaming twilight,
Farther away from the celestial
Hour by hour—
Earlobe, freckle, sphincter—
So I might mouth its maker.

EFFATA

—the word Christ spoke to the blind man,
Stroking both eyes with spit-damp clay,
His voice imperative, never to be
Disobeyed...
                    the beggar birth-blind,

Left to marvel at leaf-light, pollen,
Rainfall, the blunt bodies of birds,
And that first face, the face
Of the One who unveiled his eyes,

Jesu and His command
                                        Look! Behold! Discern!
On endless loop inside his brain, the man
Afraid to shut his eyes, to sleep, even
To blink for fear of the loss of Heaven,

Christ gone, and no one near or far
To horror miracle into his ear.

TABLE ON THE EDGE OF THE WORLD

Those days I would catch the ferry to Santorini
Just to sit at the table at Franco's, the table
Closest to the edge of the cliff. Barely
Big enough to hold an ashtray & glass,
Tiled & tilted & square,
It perched above the sea like a prow.
If I looked straight ahead, not at the caldera
Biding time below, I'd see
Nothing but air merging with the Aegean,
The horizon invisible, water & sky
Swirled into a primal blue boutique cocktail.
Behind me the world unfurled its cloak
As I leaned forward, unzipping the ether,
The velocity of vision speeding me
Away from the languor of my body.
Soon enough I lowered my gaze.
Donkeys hauled luggage up from the harbor,
Flies befouling their rheumy eyes.
That afternoon I read again the tattered volume
Of Cavafy, then slid it onto the shelf
Chalked Take One Leave One
And thumbed a book with a shattered spine,
The Confessions of Zeno by Italo Svevo, which
I rucksacked back by evening ferry
To the stone cottage & my wife's company.
Kerosene lamp. Well water.
I wondered how long we might live so simply.
I loved the novel for its quirky humor,
For its narrator's conflicted conscience

Which in its vanity mirrored my own.
Those days of the '80s have receded
Like wheel ruts below the silted seabed,
Stone roads leading nowhere
Once the volcano blackened pagan skies.
Wherever we live, some part of us dies.
Not long ago I returned to Franco's,
The bar familiar yet not the same,
As I was not the same though once again
Reading Svevo, whose book I'd tossed
Into my backpack before leaving home.
At the whim of gods
Untroubled by conscience, I finished the novel
There at that table on the edge of the world
Before returning it, damaged but intact,
To its exact spot on the shelf, itself
Imperishable down the decades,
Like the sky, the sea, the intoxicant air.

BEAUTY IN THE WORLD

So much beauty in the world… trills Macy Gray
And the studio crew claps rhythmically
Into the mic
clap clap clap clap clap clap clap
As though the response to beauty should be applause,
As in fact it was each summer evening in the '80s
At the outdoor café on the cliff on Ios
Where the rousing final movement of Dvořák
Was synced to the sun's declension
So that the orchestra crescendoed
Then abruptly ceased at the precise moment
The amaranthine disc of sun
Dissolved into the Aegean,
All of us burnt and stoned and giddy
As we burst into applause
Before nimbling the goat paths to hostels
Where we showered in anticipation
Of the modest debaucheries of night.
But it's the applause that stays with me
Rather than the ravers on holiday
In their sheer linens and seamless tans,
The applause and the beauty
That provoked it, the sunset
So elemental in that sparse landscape, the inexhaustible
Swyving of sun and sea, the hissing
We thought we heard below the cellos
And violas and tympani
Less the devil's beckoning tongue
Than the sizzle of skin, perversely

Pleasurable, more than enough
Sacrifice for our sins as we stared all day
At each other's bodies then entered them
Each night, that sibilant *pssst* louder
As flesh touched flesh in imitation
Of sun and sea, in homage to sun and sea,
To so much beauty in the world, O
Macy Gray, I'm clapping along right now
Stopped at the traffic light
Years and miles away from the island
Which still blazes in beauty without me,
Even at this hour when all the young fuckers
Who have followed my hoofprints
Sigh in their sleep
And the sun slips out of the sea
With no one watching, not one
Lost sylph searching for her sandal
Or ghost of shepherd
Or farmer on donkey to begin this day
With the joyful prayer of applause.

AMERICAN SONGBOOK

The red-tailed hawk twigged together its nest
On a ledge overlooking Central Park
Where in first-light April hours it savaged
Juvenile squirrels and blind, star-nosed moles,
And one dusk swooped to talon a pigeon
Scrounging among jouncy, bug-eyed dealers
Who flashed tin-foiled wares in Washington Square.
Binocular'd birders thrilled to each kill.
Soon city papers reported raptors
Everywhere—you had only to glance up
To find bandages of sky slashed with wings
Or shut away subway rumble to hear
Hatchlings shrill like toy factory whistles.
Some neighbors preferred the more common birds,
Mourning doves, vesper sparrows, thrushes, wrens,
And began to feed these communal choirs.
Susannah McCorkle spotted the hawk
Gliding past the river's indifference
Through the window of her 16th floor flat
As she rehearsed lush, romantic ballads—
As Time Goes By   *My Funny Valentine*
Autumn in New York   *Come Rain or Come Shine.*
The songs soothed her throat like whiskey and smoke,
But also burned, their lyrics so deeply
Incised in her body that a single,
Fevered word—*stardust*—probed some childhood wound.
She undid herself standard by standard.
They Can't Take That Away from Me, she sang,
Until rain remembered to draw a breath;

She crooned *Someone to Watch Over Me....*
One sparrow worrying the hawk's shadow
Circled tarred rooftops on West 86th.
When Susannah McCorkle leapt away
From dawn's unshakeable melancholy,
The sudden displacement of sodden air
Huffed each feather; that bird hesitated,
Then ruptured the upswell for the final
Fistful of seed still heaped upon her sill.

d. May 19, 2001

OLD SCHOOL

Seth wrestled the Camaro with one fist & popped
Handfuls of pills while the pistol rode my thigh.
I shouted *Is it loaded?* over Grandmaster Flash.
Amateur thug, he slipped the piece into his boot
& swaggered like a bouncer into the funeral home.

Sunglass'd still & jittery, he scanned the room,
Swept past uncles to the open coffin, knelt there,
Then wedged the gun between our father's thumbs,
Insurance for the celestial joyride, & tattooed,
Pierced, & fucked up, bowed his shaven skull & wept.

TIC TAC TOE

My son's Xs resemble swastikas
In his Tic Tac Toe boxes. Only four,

He's unaware of any history
Other than his own, disinterested

In a universe that doesn't hold him
At its vaginal and radiant core.

I let him win once more, my wobbly Os
Each a contracting galaxy, ready

To be rid of me. Futureless father…
While a fathergone future gyres his way.

卐 卐 卐   † † †   XXX   O
No symbol he pencils can make me stay.

SIXTIES SONNET

I have become handsome in my old age.

“You’re cute,” smiled Denise, breaking up with me,
“But cute is all you’ll ever be.”

Denise who was so wrongwrongwrong, I miss
Our Woodstock nights, half-a-million thumb-flicked

Bics coaxed to climax by God’s thwapping bass,
Hissing soppy Oms against the cloudmass.

A drenched, naked hillside soulless and pure,
Zonked, mud-caked, Yanomamö, immature.

I forgive Sly and the Family Stone.
I slept through Santana, dreaming future

Exes who might love me despite my rage.
I have grown lonesome in my afflictions.

I have become handsome in my old age.

WHITE STORK

Ciconia ciconia

Such jazzy arrhythmia,
                                        the white storks'
Plosive and gorgeous leave-takings suggest
Oracular utterance where the blurred
Danube disperses its silts.
                                        Then the red-
Billed, red-legged creatures begin to spiral,
To float among thermals like the souls, wrote
Pythagoras, praising the expansive
Grandeur of black-tipped wings, of dead poets.
Most Eastern cultures would not allow them
To be struck, not with slung stone or arrow
Or, later, lead bullet—
                                        birds who have learned,
While living, to keep their songs to themselves,
Who return to nests used for centuries,
Nests built on rooftops, haystacks, telegraph
Poles, on wooden wagon wheels placed on cold
Chimneys by peasants who hoped to draw down
Upon plague-struck villages such winged luck.

If the body in its failure remains
A nest, if the soul chooses to return…

Yet not one stork has been born in Britain
Since 1416, the last nest renounced
When Julian of Norwich, anchoress,

Having exhausted all revelations,
Took earthly dispensation, that final
Stork assuring, even while vanishing,
"Sin is behovely, but all shall be well."

RIO SAVEGRE

Tamarindo
Costa Rica

Where the Pacific seized the river, tugged
Limbs then torso toward murkier waters,
I turned back, struggled briefly, tore a path
Through the thousand frayed sienna ribbons.
I fought toward scabbed boys jabbering Spanish,
Waving skinny arms like burnt tindersticks.
I'd wanted to cross to the cloistered beach
Where turtles oared ashore to bury eggs.
That night I learned what the voices counseled:
Where salt and fresh waters tumble and stir,
Shark and crocodile sunder together.
I was lucky to leave that turbid bath.
Now I awaken when church bells worry
To recall my shade taken by current,
Riven on the waters' skin, wrenched apart
Black rag by black rag, as the soul is torn,
The heart bitten, as I stumble away,
Too dumb to know which creatures seethe below
And how whitely the body must beckon.

THE BELLS

Sanctuary Basilica
Malta

Pale novitiates flocked the bell tower
To shadow my wife one rooftop below.
Oiled, asleep, she remained unaware
Of cassock-clad boys pivoting the ledge
Until the priest appeared to knell their shame
The precise moment—punctual sinner—
I bumped open the rooftop door, bearing
In each fist a flute, orange fizz daubing
The blistered tar, the riotous mimosas
Two more slender flames expanding the near
Suburbs of hell where she sprawled, naked, stunned
Speechless on gaudy towels, below breathless
Boys, riding the pitch, not so far from God.

MAN IN BLACK

June Carter Cash, d. May 15, 2003

Why Noah summoned two of each creature
Poses no puzzle to any sentient
Breather. The dove hunched on a knobby branch
Misses his mate, though still coos all morning,
And the fat cat prowls the feather-strewn lawn
As if God lay hidden among fallen
Needles. Six kittens caper behind her.
Inside the house, I allow the lonesome
Sound of Vassar Clements' antique fiddle
To trick the wound into thinking it has
Healed. Always this sense of forward motion
Only to be pulled up short like the hound
Blustering wildly against his taut chain.
No heaven but in the momentary
Glimpse of sunlight on iridescent breast,
Or in the note silked on air as horsehair
Caresses gut, sending forth its blue throb
Into the churchy silence between barks.
When I step outside, I can't remember
Spring—the world's hushed now, anticipating
Waters that will pummel the green earth flat
And the one dove who'll fly off not knowing
If he can find an exposed mountain peak
Or, come nightfall, make it back to the ark.

Johnny Cash, d. September 12, 2003

DIOGENES

The water lay flat to the horizon and so clear
You could swim far out past the coral reef
And, looking down, still see the sandy shelf
Tilting below pale, coffin-shaped feet.
Barracuda hung like mobiles in the blue layers,
Cool gunmetal, unwavering, purposeful.
The days were long, and I wanted nothing,
Though sometimes I thought I wanted truth
Until the burning, colorless liqueurs confused me.
I was grateful for their little brushfires in my body.
The days were long, yes, and growing longer.
I strolled through the evening throngs,
The tourists in loud shirts and straw hats,
And dined alone among them while ancient,
Indigenous men bearing guitars and whittled flutes
Shuffled table to table, birthing once more
That one, lilting, Incan melody everyone hums.
In the morning, when clumps of flies
Blackened honeyed scrolls tacked to rafters,
When truth prodded me again
With its trumpet blare of heat and light,
I snorkeled toward families of green squid,
Alert, throbbing, horizontal, lit-from-within
Coke bottles teasing me forth
As if I could unloosen my skin
Like a shirt forgotten on the beach
To be borne away at night by lapping waters,
As if I might join those inky creatures
To spend my days reaching always for the nothing
That remains just beyond my grasp.

BLACK SEA SPA

Neptun, Romania

Not nude exactly, pajama'd in mud,
The grandfathers stood like unlovely trees
Crooking bare branches as our train curved past,
The century flown forward without them.
A bean field away the old women swayed,
Furrowed bellies and breasts daubed like birds' nests,
A fairy-tale forest of breathing bark
Summoned by spell or tribal ritual,
A final spasm of pagan pleasure.
Mesmerized too, we gazed from the window,
Returning waves, their scythed, crescent gestures,
Their mute acknowledgment of time passing
As mud hardened and only eyes or lips
Or the spark of one pink fingertip glowed
In irradiated, Chernobyl dusk.
Surreal, you muttered, but forced a wave
As we were mirrored in glass streaked with grit
And struck at each curve by sunset's stutter,
As though the hammer still fell on this last
Generation to have suffered world war,
Who heal themselves by interring themselves
In curative earth before the last death.

DEAD IRAQIS

On our balcony, two Iraqis are eating a dead Iraqi
That has ruffled in rain for three days, one more dead Iraqi
Beginning slow dissolution until only feathers remain.
Some plague has infected the city—dead Iraqis
Litter rooftops, and sick Iraqis like ripped petticoats remain
Underfoot, dazed, or remain
On roadways till crushed by trucks. Those dead Iraqis
Are eaten in ragged cotillions; soon more dead Iraqis
Befoul schoolyards and parks. Children kick dead Iraqis
Like soccer balls, explosive bursts of feathers, dead Iraqis
Pinwheeling in air where almost no live Iraqis remain.
For the first few days it didn't register: dead Iraqis
High and low. Everywhere you looked, dead Iraqis.
Then like a poem startling in its clarity: *Oh! The Iraqis. Dead.*

MICHELANGELO MERISI DA CARAVAGGIO

The Beheading of St. John
1608

The Baptist's beheaded Arab fashion:
Throat slit with the long sword, then the gristly
Tendons of the neck severed with the knife
Still sheathed behind this executioner's
Back—the beheading's not quite over yet,
Like the tape loop broadcast on CNN:
Al-Qaeda zealots crisscrossed with bullets
Posing with the blindfolded journalist
Before the anonymous assassin
Steps forward to undertake his righteous
Labor. On websites the tape winds forward
To the crass, theatrical brandishing
Of the skull, another obscene gesture
In a war targeted toward spectacle.
Two prisoners gape from their somber cell.
The girl-servant grips the copper platter
Upon which the head will be presented
To Salomè. Blood puddles the stone floor
Where, aswirl, it twists into the artist's
Only surviving signature, *Michel*,
To confess his helpless complicity.

BELOVED

Romania
1989

She cradles the rag-swathed, 40-watt bulb
Like a hand-painted egg in woolen gloves
With holes scissored at forefinger and thumb
For turning pages in the icy nook.
The library looms beyond gritty drifts,
Past blood-soaked slats and the empty, grease-glossed
Hooks beckoning from butcher shop windows.
Last week she began reading *Ethan Frome*,
A donated copy—some Fulbright prof's—
And felt that New England snowscape her own,
But the volume's vanished between visits.
She hopes Ethan chose love over duty.
Still, she can't bring herself to steal a book;
Ceauşescu won't be shot until Christmas.
She scours shelves for American novels—
Overhead bulbs fizzled out years ago—
Then finds the harrowing tale of a slave
That makes her bulb seem to surge with power
Hour after hour in the cold cubicle.
(A decade later she'll meet the author.)
Sixteen now, she can't anticipate much,
Except to be loved as she loves these books.

for Mihaela

YOUNG JOHN CLARE

Helpston, Northamptonshire, 1806

Not often do I find a nest fallen
Among seed pods in autumn, three blue-white
Eggs broken, rags of rucked and yellow flesh
And hinge of beak still beckoning ants, but
One egg sealed, the fluids of birdmaking
A milky galaxy bundled inside—
So smooth and dry I want to swivel it
Wholly into my mouth despite dirt-flecks,
Lave the vowel-sheen off the oval shell,
Tumble that globule of starling within
Until its unspooled trill begins to boil,
Slips its bony case and kindles my voice.
O then would I sing! I would have no choice.

ALCHEMY

Familiar words suddenly became strange,
Confusing him—not so much their meanings,
But their characters, the letters themselves—
Some quirk of the eyesight, less a loss
Of language than its transformation,
Ovidian, the marks writhing while read,
Poetry, perhaps, bewitched to *burlap*:
The *p* suddenly tumbled upside down,
The clasps of *o* and *e* opened—*u r*—
Then the *t-r-y* become *l-a-p*
Uncrossed, doubled up, pinched shut faced forward
Respectively, devilishly—the word
Less abstract, assuming texture and heft,
Rough to the touch, less a bolt of lightning
Than bolt of cloth woven to bind the book.

THE TEMPEST

19th C

Each plush box, tier upon tier,
Furnished a stage-side gilt wall mirror
Tilted at a precise angle
So patrons might eyeball each arrival
With faux disinterest.
The great European theatres are gone,
Ruined by war, by fire, by general ennui.
Gone are the stagehands, always too poor
To seat their children in the gallery,
Who cranked the handle of the wind machine,
Opened and closed the drawers of the rain box,
And swept the thunder roller over the wooden floor
So even magistrates in orchestra seats
Glanced upward more than once.
Later a father would tell his brood
How Prospero walled his cave with books,
Or—better yet—how from the catwalk
He observed the anemic chaplain
Tongue a coin of spittle
Off the epaulet of the sleeping corporal.

BLACK OLIVES

In those days while my then-wife
Taught English to a mustached young nurse who hoped to join
Her uncle's practice in Queens,
I'd sip gin on our balcony and listen to her
Read aloud from the phrasebook,
Then hear the student mimic, slowly, *Where does it hurt?*
Then my wife repeat those words
So the woman might enunciate each syllable,
Until I could no longer
Bear it, so I'd prowl the Ambelokipi district
Attempting to decipher
Titles emblazoned on marquees—*My Life As A Dog,*
Runaway Train, Raging Bull—
Then stroll past dark shops that still sold only one item—
Kerosene, soap, cheese, notebooks—
To step down into the shop that sold olives, only
Olives in barrels riddling
A labyrinth of dank aisles and buttressing brick walls.
I'd sidle among squat drums,
Fingering the fruit, thumbing their inky shine, their rucked
Skins like blistered fingertips,
Their plump flesh, the rough salts needling them, judging their cowled
Heft, biding my time. Always
I'd select a half-kilo of the most misshapen,
Wrinkled and blackest olives
Sprung from the sacred rubble below Mt. Athos, then
Had to shout "Fuck Kissinger!"
Three times before the proprietor would allow me
To make my purchase, then step

Back out into the smut-stirred Athens night to begin
The slow stroll home, bearing now
My little sack of woe, oil seeping through brown paper,
Each olive brought toward my mouth
Mirroring lights flung from marquees and speeding taxis,
Each olive burning its coal-
Flame of bitterness and history into my tongue.

FAUNS FLEEING BEFORE AN AUTOMOBILE

What young couple, leaving the affair, hasn't seen them,
The fauns, leaping vast foliaged silences,
Slashed momentarily by headlights:
Their yellow, goatlike, sin-slit eyes,
Their scabrous haunches,
The dull gloss of cloven hoof as it disappears in brush?

We had been arguing, slightly drunk,
About ex-lovers with flirtatious
Gestures, about low murmurs in corners—
Suddenly they appeared, three or four,
A muscular rush among brambles, a furious blur, almost-
Human creatures swept underworld by light.

Our rampant voices stilled then—
That awestruck *hush*,
Creation's tentative pause—
Then only the tick of wipers urging our arrival
Home, the undressing, the desperate
Confusions of flesh—mine or yours?—

While fauns huddled in leaf shadow,
Rubbing together their burr-riddled, filth-smeared
Flanks, nuzzling coarse necks, still
Spooked by the splendor
Kindling God's wild eyes, still
Catching their terrible breath.

POINCIANA

The man who offered one hundred dollars
To watch me undress my wife wasn't pocked
Or breathy like some B-movie voyeur,
But had approached us in the hotel bar
And improvised almost perfect English.
His burnished leather loafers and blazer
Sparked elegance amid rumpled shirttails
And parrot-hued, flimsy sheaths and sandals.
Tipsy from fingers of flaming liqueurs
That beckon only in foreign countries,
Sun-flushed and giddy with tropical spunk,
We let him swim the runnel of perfume
Coursing the lobby, leading to our room.
On our balcony, I unzipped her dress,
Slipped it off shoulders to expose her breasts—
Then pool at her feet in a tinsel shimmer
As though she were stepping like Susannah
From her garden bath of spices and oils.
Whose fantasy this was, I can't recall.
The man knelt on tiles, weeping from one eye.
My nude wife trembled in jazz-laden breeze.
I tapped one finger along the ivory
Keys of her spine, not knowing what came next,
Or how to strike our shame
Before money exchanged hands
Or when waking next morning wild with thirst.

WEDDING DRESS

That Halloween I wore your wedding dress,
Our children spooked & wouldn't speak for days.
I'd razored taut calves smooth, teased each blown tress,
Then—lipsticked, mascara'd, & self-amazed—
Shimmied like a starlet on the dance floor.
I'd never felt so sensual before—
Catholic schoolgirl & neighborhood whore.
In bed, dolled up, undone, we fantasized:
We clutched & fused, torn twins who'd been denied.
You were my shy groom. Love, I was your bride.

AMERICAN EEL

Anguilla rostrata

My quick & kindling daughter
Bolted ahead as we approached the abandoned wharf,
Light flashing off burial
Mounds slick with silt & salt marshes raveling the bay.
We were not quite family.
My lover had flown down from New England, elegant
In haute couture even here
Among bridle paths & planks warping over runnels,
Spiked heels daubed with mud, bangles
Chiming like birdcall, each gesture sparked & erratic,
The air barbed with a coursing
Electricity, a nervous energy that drew
Admirers into its light,
Then burned them, as she exhausted herself & her friends
With helpless consummations.
"We're not that kind of people," she'd admonish her son,
Who propped one elbow upon
The table or let a shirttail droop, then lick her thumb
To rub away a freckle.
Suddenly my daughter let loose a shrill *ewwww!*—we heard,
Below that sour pitch, a dim
Sorption like soapsuds sieving through a wooden bucket:
Eels stranded in low tide, mud
Eels thrashing the river's bottom, urging their flaccid
Intimations forward inch
By blunt inch before doubling back on themselves, tugging
Their viscous sleeves through throbbing
Clumps of sisters tangled like fishing line. Creation's

Rank exhalations—the eels'
Frenzied upheavals & shudderings—freighted the air.
"Let's get the fuck outta here!"
Yelped my daughter. My fiancée glared, then turned away
To let me wrestle the flaw.
Speckled paths & murmurous streams recalled the famous
Forest scene: Dimmesdale reveling
In arousal when he quit the moral wilderness
Where Hester Prynne had undone
Her hair to allow its sexual waters to bathe him,
The reverend ready to teach
Puritan children how to curse, or torch the virgin's
Innocence with some verbal
"Germ of evil," one coarse utterance to make her flinch.
"Bad word," I wagged my finger
As my daughter looked chastened, as my lover eased back
Into our perfect future,
"But"—I couldn't help myself—"you used it correctly."
I hugged my girl, my darling
Vulgarity. We *are* that kind of people. Eels seethed,
Convulsive balls of gristle,
Then boiled through mud flats to rupture the river's veneer.

COMMERCE

Niagara Falls
18—

Some half-wit Barnum, amateur Noah,
Fashioned an ark—a salvaged, broken barge—
To populate with creatures trapped or bought:
Black bear, wolverine, a fox like a flame,

Peacocks, possum, hogs, raccoon, wailing tribe
Of forsaken dogs, weasel, skunk, even—
According to eyewitness reports—six
Silver monkeys shipped by rail from New York,

God's mange-thumbed menagerie chained to planks
That would have floated three runaway slaves
Had not abolitionists threatened court.
Then Noah bid his bestiary good-bye,

The raft of lamentation set adrift,
Its creatures more confused than crazed, almost
Calm as the ark spiraled toward the maelstrom,
The waters' vast uproar drowning weak cries,

White mists like shrouds enveloping the crew
While spectators whooped and scrambled both banks
And newsboys shilled beer a nickel a glass
Till it perched midair on the precipice....

Folklore swears the bear survived, pummeled ashore
Where men beat her with clubs and muzzled her,
Then dragged that rough beast saloon to saloon
Where drafts of whiskey were chugged down her throat.

By morning she lay a rank heap on State—
Schoolchildren leapfrogged the raggedy corpse.
Then one cat was found, eyeless, legs broken,
So for the next decade tramps tortured strays

To sell them to tourists, farm boys, and Poles
As The Cat Swept Over Niagara Falls,
Singular souvenir, His living hand,
New World miracle—only one dollar.

SCARABS

Coleoptera scarabaeidae

...their representations used in ancient Egypt
as symbols of resurrection

Red dirt pummeled by goat-herd generations
Plumes the path bearing our sandal soles' impress
Till rain feathers flat each warped hourglass.

And who are we?—twin nobodies
Unsung in the untranslatable sagas,
Abandoned in the ongoing odysseys.

Vipers tongue our noon-stunted shades.
Like savage forebears, we dwell upon the dirt
Where beetles, green-black glints, each a mini-

Sisyphus, commence their crucial business:
Turning the earth so that torrents of light
Sweep vast provinces into the future...

Where, palsied and riven by syphilis,
We no longer recognize our ravaged
Faces, or recall lush gardens of our making.

How will I find you once I awaken,
Crawling from caverns, blinded by sun,
Naked amid the alien thistle,

No longer speaking our common tongue?—
While dazzling drudges, jeweled citizens,
Tumble forward their terrible burdens,

Rotating newly formed planets of dung.

BALTHUS

When the angel arrived, bare-breasted, androgynous,
Its lower half sheathed in tulle
Bluer than the plums in ceramic bowls propped on stools,
The vetch in the studio
Revived; colors assumed blunt authority; even
Yellow became heavy. Bells
Tolled from tinny speakers: Mozart striking precise notes
With an almost disarming
Simplicity, their grace and gravity suggesting
The long marriage of pleasure
And sorrow. *Così fan tutte.* I named the angel
Katia, thus assigning
Gender. Now each brushstroke resonates with tumescence.
Black mirror, red table, moth,
White skirt. *Nude in Front of a Mantel. Girl on Her Knees.*
Sprawled on a chair, Katia
Pretends to read a volume of sonnets by Rilke.
I pencil in my journal:
To assume God's face, to ponder what He incarnates:
Landscape, young girls' flesh, newly
Ripe spring fruits, trees full of sap, the sweetness of sleeping
Children. I know that this work—
A painter's required labor—always means redemption.
When I look up, the angel
Has fallen asleep, but the plums, those taut plums bursting
Flecked skins, have been devoured.

PAVESE

Cesare Pavese (b. 1908) committed suicide on August 27, 1950. His relationship with American actress Constance Dowling had ended. Nine days earlier he had written the final entry in his diary: "I will not write anymore."

I inhabit this body, Don Niccolo dé Pelagati,
As you inhabited for weeks the iron cage
Suspended above the filthy streets of Ferrara, 1495.
Birds convened their solemn judiciary.
Once you snared a pigeon by its talon,
Then ate it still living, morsel by feathery morsel,
Its frantic heart pumping blood into your mouth.
The merciless sun seared your skin,
Each blister a tiny Vatican.
At night the northern wind whipped you with its icy lash.
When you died, one yellow eye
Spilled onto the street; your flesh rotted to rags.
Still you swayed above commerce and pageantry,
Raining lightly onto cobblestones:
A shriveled ear, a shrunken thumb, what remained of your sex
Puddling below for rats to tongue.
I suffer this body, forefather, doubter,
As your living body and unregenerate corpse
Suffered its iron cage.
Already I have become one of the old men
Who endures each day without love.
Non scriverò piú.
I rage in your remnants and stains.

BLUE ANKLE

That stooped old woman who tremors through Kieślowski's films
Takes almost an hour, it seems,
To heft one milk carton into the recycling bin,
Groaning her arm up only
So high so long, failing again to push the plastic
Through the rubber-flanged circle
Of the public receptacle.
And the young woman's
Always watching. Should she leave
The window to help the woman slip the container
Into the drop or flutter
Her letter—in another sequence, another film—
Toward the narrow mailbox slot?
One friend half-jokes that we're all coming to a bad end.
Is the arthritic woman
Some future version of herself, blue ankle swollen,
Spine hunched like a question mark,
Drab woolen coat too thin to repel the frost-edged wind,
Scarf askew, the few whiskers
Poking from her chin like the black spikes of sea urchins?
And after she releases,
At last, the empty jug into the receptacle,
Where does she go?—to which cramped
Studio along which pocked lane where art school dropouts
Loiter, racing engines, sleek
Cycles propped on the sidewalk so she's forced to weave through
A labyrinth of chrome and fumes
To reach her door, then ascend steep steps to the fifth floor?
Mercifully, Kieślowski's

Camera doesn't accompany her.
Nor have we seen
One of those boys, as a joke,
Not meaning to hit her, lob a loose cobble, striking
The woman's ankle so fire
Sears up her leg, but she drags her foot forward without
Turning, the boys dumbfounded,
Embarrassed now, till the one who tossed the stone, almost
As an afterthought, shouts "Jew!"—
Then the rest scoop up fistfuls of rubble and warn her
To keep moving, though no one
Tosses another stone, and the woman feels too much
Pain to allow consciousness
Its thorny, inexhaustible registry of fear.
All coming to a bad end. . . .
Dominika turns from snow-struck glass back to her room
Where her lover smokes in bed.
He seems vain, superfluous now, though she once enjoyed
Encircling his waist, pressing
Her cheek against the cold black leather of his jacket
That smelled of gas and absinthe
While the cycle surged Warsaw's crooked passageways, once
Took pleasure in their vulgar
Colleagues who preened, crow-like, uncircumcised cocks erect,
As she sketched them for art class.
Her mother's dead ten years. Her father's letters bear stamps
From a distant country, so
This boy's the only one who holds her these days, these nights
All coming to a bad end
Though later she will dream the woman rinsing one dish
Or watching soap operas fling
Vertical corpses across blank windows while she soothes

Her bruised ankle with chipped ice,
With a gentleness no lover has ever possessed.

NOTES

The epigraphs to this collection are from *Moby-Dick; or, The Whale* by Herman Melville (1851) and *The Adventures of Huckleberry Finn* by Mark Twain (1885), respectively.

"After the Argument": the lines quoted as epigraph are from "Suzanne" by John Logan in *The Collected Poems* (Brockport, NY: Boa Editions, 1989).

"American Songbook": jazz singer Susannah McCorkle recorded numerous albums of popular standards and performed at Carnegie Hall and Lincoln Center, as well as at cabarets, such as The Cookery in Greenwich Village. We met at Yaddo in 1983.

"Apatite": for Jan Beatty. The Geminids meteor shower, an annual event, occurs in mid-December.

"Ashkenazi Birthmark": triggered, in part, by the essay "We Tell Ourselves Stories in Order to Live Again" in *Make It Scream, Make It Burn* (New York: Little, Brown and Company, 2019) by Leslie Jamison and, in part, by the iconic and haunting photograph, known as The Last Jew in Vinnitsa, taken during the Holocaust, possibly in April 1942, in Ukraine. Once when I was twenty, I thought that I was dying and, in my terror, saw above me a swirling column, a tornado in which my ancestors hovered, singing, face after face funneling upward into the distant past, and that tornado touched down precisely on the birthmark on my forehead, calming me. My father was Irish Catholic, and I was raised in the Catholic faith, but my mother was Jewish. This poem, written a half-century after that visitation, connects my birthmark to my maternal ancestors.

"Balthus": *in memoriam Balthasar Klossowski, d. February 18, 2001*: the italicized lines appear, in slightly different form, in his memoir, *Vanished Splendors*, as told to Alaín Vircondelet, trans. Benjamin Ivry (Ecco, 2002). Several other lines are drawn from this source.

"Beauty in the World": the song of that title appears on *The Sellout* (2010) by Macy Gray, lyrics and melody by Macy Gray, music by Josh Lopez, George Reichart and Kannon Kross, handclaps by Jared Lee Gosselin, Phillip White and Shelton Rivers.

"Blue Ankle": *in memoriam Krzysztof Kieślowski, d. March 13, 1996*: Polish filmmaker whose films include *Decalogue, The Double Life of Veronique,* and *Three Colors*: *Blue, White, Red.* Triggered by a recurring scene, the poem does not focus on any single film.

"Classic Cocktail": my late father, a NYC firefighter, tended bar at the Starlight Lounge in Hempstead, Long Island, in the '60s. The poem recalls Connie Francis' 1959 hit, "Lipstick on Your Collar."

"Clean Asshole Poem": the sentence by Chekhov appears in *Notebook of Anton Chekhov*, trans. S.S. Koteliansky & Leonard Woolf (Ecco, 1987). The full title of Peter Orlovsky's book is *Clean Asshole Poems & Smiling Vegetable Songs* (City Lights, 1978). In October 1966, when I was sixteen, I met Peter Orlovsky & Allen Ginsberg after Ginsberg's poetry reading at Town Hall in NYC. The couple invited me back to their apartment for soup. I regret that I declined.

"Dead Iraqis": for Jeffrey Skinner. On April 23, 2009, The Associated Press reported that more than 110,600 Iraqis have died in violence since the 2003 U.S.-led invasion. The number is a minimum count of violent deaths. The official who provided the data, on condition of anonymity due to its sensitivity, estimated the actual number of deaths at ten to twenty percent higher because of thousands who are still missing and civilians who were buried without official records.

"Effata": for Gail Langstroth, eurythmist.

"Fauns Fleeing Before an Automobile": Beneš Knüpfer, oil on canvas, 1905, Museum of Modern Art, Prague.

"Magdalene": a photograph of Donatello's sculpture, with commentary, appears in *Glittering Images* by Camille Paglia (New York: Pantheon Books, 2012). The sculpture is exhibited in the Museo dell'Opera del Duomo, Florence, Italy.

"Man in Black": Vassar Clements (1928-2005) was one of the world's finest fiddlers. His recordings include "High Lonesome Sound," "Lonesome Fiddler Blues," and "'Til the End of the World Rolls 'Round." His fiddle, probably built by Gaspar Duiffoprugcar in the late 1500s, was decorated with unusual carvings and paintings, including one of Sappho holding a lute.

"Michelangelo Merisi da Caravaggio": The painting hangs in St. John's Co-Cathedral in Valetta, Malta. The word "assassin" is derived via French from the Arabic *ha ā īn*, literally "hashish users," denoting a group of 11th Century Ismaili Muslims who murdered Christian leaders.

"Misericord": photographs of mercy seats, with commentary, appear in *A Little Book of Misericords* by Mike Harding (London, UK: Aurum Press Ltd., 1998).

"Pavese": Don Niccolo dé Pelagati was locked in an iron cage outside the tower of San Giuliano on August 12, 1495. A priest, he had committed numerous crimes, including murder.

"Pedestrian Mall": with a nod to "Young Goodman Brown" (1835) by Nathaniel Hawthorne.

"Performance Artist": in memory of visual artist Robbie Tillotson (1949-1987): the epigraph is from HIV InSite of the University of California-San Francisco Center for HIV Information: http://hivinsite.ucsf.edu/InSite?page=kb-01-03#S1.4X

"Poinciana": a tropical tree bearing orange and red blossoms. Also the title of the influential jazz recording released in 1951 by pianist Ahmad Jamal.

"Red-Billed Firefinch": epigraph: "Absolution, With a Wing and a Prayer" by Jaime Yaya Barry, *The New York Times*, October 5, 2016. These finches are also known as "birds of forgiveness."

"*Self-Portrait with Doll* (1920-21)": the title of a painting by Oskar Kokoschka. There are accounts of this doll online and in print, including one in Robert Hughes' *Nothing If Not Critical* (Penguin, 1992). Several online accounts display photographs of the doll.

"Sixties Sonnet": anthropologist Napoleon A. Chagnon, in a letter to *The New York Times Magazine* (March 3, 2013), writes: "I object to the notion that whether the tribe I studied is called 'Yanomamö' or 'Yanomami' is a matter of preference. It is a matter of linguistics. The final vowel /ö/ in Yanomamö is important; some people don't hear it and therefore cannot pronounce the name that the Yanomamö use for themselves.

If the name is rendered 'Yanomami,' people pronounce it 'Yanoma-meee.' This mispronunciation can be traced to members of the Catholic missions in Venezuela and Brazil who came from countries where Romance languages are spoken and had trouble hearing the final vowel /ö/. The rendition of the tribal name as 'Yanomami' gives me an uncomfortable feeling that I am subscribing to and endorsing a 500-year legacy of Spanish, Portuguese and French colonialism among Native Americans in the New World. I hope outsiders will take this into consideration when they adopt a spelling for the tribal name." Okay. Peace.

"The Tempest": The Manoel Theatre in Valetta, Malta, built in 1731 for the Knights of St. John, remains active. Its museum houses the 19th century sound equipment.

"Trivia Night at Kiki's Beach Bar": if you wonder wonder who… who wrote "The Book of Love," recorded by The Monotones, it was written by Warren Davis, George Malone and Charles Patrick, three members of that doo-wop group. The song reached #5 on the *Billboard* pop chart in 1958.

"White Stork": *Revelations of Divine Love* by Julian of Norwich (1342-c.1416) is believed to be the first book written by a woman in the English language. T.S. Eliot samples the quoted passage at greater length in "Little Gidding" from *Four Quartets.*

"Young John Clare": In 1806, John Clare, then thirteen, bought James Thomson's poem, *The Seasons*, which inspired him to become a poet.

ACKNOWLEDGMENTS

Warm thanks for their generous support to the editors and staff of the journals in which the new poems, sometimes in earlier versions, appeared:

Alaska Quarterly Review: "The Afterlife";
America: "Gethsemane";
Arts & Letters: "After the Argument," "Pagan Sky";
Bennington Review: "Otherworld";
Brilliant Corners: "Late Piano Lesson";
Chautauqua: "Magdalene";
The Gettysburg Review: "Ashkenazi Birthmark," "Natural Habitat," "Spousal Sonnet";
The Greensboro Review: "Palmistry";
James Dickey Review: "Brooklyn Limbo," "Dirt Devil";
North American Review: "Parable," "Pedestrian Mall";
Phi Kappa Phi Forum: "Gwendolyn Brooks," "Report from October";
Poetry Northwest: "To a Thief Who Died Young";
Salt: "Mount Hope Cemetery";
Southern Indiana Review: "Visitation";
This Broken Shore: "Brooklyn Showdown," "Human Dance," "The Poisoning";
Tupelo Quarterly: "Mount Hope Cemetery" [reprint].

"Ashkenazi Birthmark" was reprinted in *The Best American Poetry 2024*, eds. Mary Jo Salter and David Lehman (Scribner, 2024).

Several poems, translated by Frances Simán, appeared in *Ærea* (Chile), *Alastor* (Nicaragua), and *El Golem* (Honduras), and were included in *Poemas ascendentes* by Michael Waters (Ecuador: El Ángel Editor, 2024) and *4625 millas* by Michael Waters and Mihaela Moscaliuc (Mexico: Universidad Autónoma de Nuevo León, 2025). Thank you, Frances, for your enthusiasm, generosity, and humor.

Some poems also appeared in *Scrisul Românesc* (Romania), translated by Carmen Firan, and in *Light Year* (China), translated by Weina Dai.

I remain grateful for a 2022 residency at the Virginia Center for the Creative Arts. Special thanks to Sheila Pleasants and Dana Jones.

Thanks too to the New Jersey State Council on the Arts for support in 2023 and 2025.

Warm thanks as well to the editors and staff of the journals in which the selected poems, sometimes in earlier versions, appeared:

The American Poetry Review, *Arts & Letters*, *Chautauqua*, *Connecticut Review*, *Copper Nickel*, *Crab Orchard Review*, *Field*, *5 A.M.*, *The Georgia Review*, *The Gettysburg Review*, *Great River Review*, *The Hopkins Review*, *The Idaho Review*, *The Kenyon Review*, *Michigan Quarterly Review*, *New Letters*, *Nine Mile*, *The Paris Review*, *Pleiades*, *Poetry*, *Poetry International*, *The Progressive*, *Shenandoah*, *Solstice*, and *The Southern Review*.

"Commerce" was reprinted in *The Pushcart Prize XXVIII*.
"Black Olives" was reprinted in *The Pushcart Prize XXXII*.
"Beloved" was reprinted in *The Pushcart Prize XXXVII*.

The selected poems have been chosen from the following books:

Sinnerman (Etruscan Press, 2023).
Caw (Boa Editions, 2020).
The Dean of Discipline (University of Pittsburgh Press, 2018).
Celestial Joyride (Boa Editions, 2016).
Gospel Night (Boa Editions, 2011).
Darling Vulgarity (Boa Editions, 2006).

"Brooklyn Walk-Up"; "Shark River Bridge"; "Prayer with Caravaggio"; and "Table on the Edge of the World" from *Sinnerman*, by Michael Waters, © 2023. Reprinted by permission of Etruscan Press.

"IEȘIRE →"; "Classic Cocktail"; "Performance Artist"; "Karakul"; and "Poetry" from *The Dean of Discipline*, by Michael Waters, © 2018. Reprinted by permission of the University of Pittsburgh Press.

For their generosity, warmth, and acumen, thank you to Philip Brady at Etruscan Press and to the late Ed Ochester at the University of Pittsburgh Press. And for the breadth of his editorial vision and his ongoing support while steering Boa into its 50th year, deep gratitude to Peter Conners at Boa Editions.

And so much love & gratitude to my family: Fabian & Kiernan; Zach; Vali, Dora, Vlad, & Ana;

& Mihaela Moscaliuc, who rewrote the Book of Love.

ABOUT THE AUTHOR

Michael Waters has published fifteen books of poetry, among them *Sinnerman* (Etruscan Press, 2023), *Caw* (Boa Editions, 2020), *The Dean of Discipline* (University of Pittsburgh Press, 2018), *Darling Vulgarity* (Boa Editions, 2006), finalist for the *Los Angeles Times* Book Prize, *Parthenopi: New and Selected Poems* (Boa Editions, 2001), finalist for the Paterson Poetry Prize, and earlier collections from Carnegie Mellon University Press. *The Bicycle and the Soul: Prose on Poetry*, appeared in 2024. He has edited/co-edited several anthologies, including *Border Lines: Poems of Migration* (Knopf, 2020) and *Contemporary American Poetry* (Houghton Mifflin, 2006). His poems have appeared in five editions of *The Pushcart Prize* and in *Best American Poetry*. He has chaired the poetry panel of the National Book Awards and been Fulbright Scholar in American Studies at Al. I. Cuza University in Iasi, Romania. Among his honors are fellowships from the John Simon Guggenheim Memorial Foundation and the National Endowment for the Arts, Individual Artist Awards from the New Jersey State Council on the Arts and the Maryland State Arts Council, and residencies at Yaddo, MacDowell, Virginia Center for the Creative Arts, Anderson Center for Interdisciplinary Studies, Tyrone Guthrie Centre (Ireland), St. James Cavalier Centre (Malta), and Chateau de Lavigny (Switzerland). He lives without a cell phone in Ocean, NJ, which shares its zip code with the much cooler Asbury Park.

BOA EDITIONS AMERICAN POETS CONTINUUM SERIES

No. 1 *The Fuhrer Bunker: A Cycle of Poems in Progress*
W. D. Snodgrass

No. 2 *She*
M. L. Rosenthal

No. 3 *Living With Distance*
Ralph J. Mills, Jr.

No. 4 *Not Just Any Death*
Michael Waters

No. 5 *That Was Then: New and Selected Poems*
Isabella Gardner

No. 6 *Things That Happen Where There Aren't Any People*
William Stafford

No. 7 *The Bridge of Change: Poems 1974–1980*
John Logan

No. 8 *Signatures*
Joseph Stroud

No. 9 *People Live Here: Selected Poems 1949–1983*
Louis Simpson

No. 10 *Yin*
Carolyn Kizer

No. 11 *Duhamel: Ideas of Order in Little Canada*
Bill Tremblay

No. 12 *Seeing It Was So*
Anthony Piccione

No. 13 *Hyam Plutzik: The Collected Poems*

No. 14 *Good Woman: Poems and a Memoir 1969–1980*
Lucille Clifton

No. 15 *Next: New Poems*
Lucille Clifton

No. 16 *Roxa: Voices of the Culver Family*
William B. Patrick

No. 17 *John Logan: The Collected Poems*

No. 18 *Isabella Gardner: The Collected Poems*

No. 19 *The Sunken Lightship*
Peter Makuck

No. 20 *The City in Which I Love You*
Li-Young Lee

No. 21 *Quilting: Poems 1987–1990*
Lucille Clifton

No. 22 *John Logan: The Collected Fiction*

No. 23 *Shenandoah and Other Verse Plays*
Delmore Schwartz

No. 24 *Nobody Lives on Arthur Godfrey Boulevard*
Gerald Costanzo

No. 25 *The Book of Names: New and Selected Poems*
Barton Sutter

No. 26 *Each in His Season*
W. D. Snodgrass

No. 27 *Wordworks: Poems Selected and New*
Richard Kostelanetz

No. 28 *What We Carry*
Dorianne Laux

No. 29 *Red Suitcase*
Naomi Shihab Nye

No. 30 *Song*
Brigit Pegeen Kelly

No. 31 *The Fuehrer Bunker: The Complete Cycle*
W. D. Snodgrass

No. 32 *For the Kingdom*
Anthony Piccione

No. 33 *The Quicken Tree*
Bill Knott

No. 34 *These Upraised Hands*
William B. Patrick

No. 35 *Crazy Horse in Stillness*
William Heyen

No. 36 *Quick, Now, Always*
Mark Irwin

No. 37 *I Have Tasted the Apple*
Mary Crow

No. 38 *The Terrible Stories*
Lucille Clifton

No. 39 *The Heat of Arrivals*
Ray Gonzalez

No. 40 *Jimmy & Rita*
Kim Addonizio

No. 41 *Green Ash, Red Maple, Black Gum*
Michael Waters

No. 42 *Against Distance*
Peter Makuck

No. 43 *The Night Path*
Laurie Kutchins

No. 44 *Radiography*
Bruce Bond

No. 45 *At My Ease: Uncollected Poems of the Fifties and Sixties*
David Ignatow

No. 46 *Trillium*
Richard Foerster

No. 47 *Fuel*
Naomi Shihab Nye

No. 48 *Gratitude*
Sam Hamill

No. 49 *Diana, Charles, & the Queen*
William Heyen

No. 50 *Plus Shipping*
Bob Hicok

No. 51 *Cabato Sentora*
Ray Gonzalez

No. 52 *We Didn't Come Here for This*
William B. Patrick

No. 53 *The Vandals*
Alan Michael Parker

No. 54 *To Get Here*
Wendy Mnookin

No. 55 *Living Is What I Wanted: Last Poems*
David Ignatow

No. 56 *Dusty Angel*
Michael Blumenthal

No. 57 *The Tiger Iris*
Joan Swift

No. 58 *White City*
Mark Irwin

No. 59 *Laugh at the End of the World: Collected Comic Poems 1969–1999*
Bill Knott

No. 60 *Blessing the Boats: New and Selected Poems: 1988–2000*
Lucille Clifton

No. 97 *Not for Specialists: New and Selected Poems*
W. D. Snodgrass

No. 98 *Splendor*
Steve Kronen

No. 99 *Woman Crossing a Field*
Deena Linett

No. 100 *The Burning of Troy*
Richard Foerster

No. 101 *Darling Vulgarity*
Michael Waters

No. 102 *The Persistence of Objects*
Richard Garcia

No. 103 *Slope of the Child Everlasting*
Laurie Kutchins

No. 104 *Broken Hallelujahs*
Sean Thomas Dougherty

No. 105 *Peeping Tom's Cabin: Comic Verse 1928–2008*
X. J. Kennedy

No. 106 *Disclamor*
G.C. Waldrep

No. 107 *Encouragement for a Man Falling to His Death*
Christopher Kennedy

No. 108 *Sleeping with Houdini*
Nin Andrews

No. 109 *Nomina*
Karen Volkman

No. 110 *The Fortieth Day*
Kazim Ali

No. 111 *Elephants & Butterflies*
Alan Michael Parker

No. 112 *Voices*
Lucille Clifton

No. 113 *The Moon Makes Its Own Plea*
Wendy Mnookin

No. 114 *The Heaven-Sent Leaf*
Katy Lederer

No. 115 *Struggling Times*
Louis Simpson

No. 116 *And*
Michael Blumenthal

No. 117 *Carpathia*
Cecilia Woloch

No. 118 *Seasons of Lotus, Seasons of Bone*
Matthew Shenoda

No. 119 *Sharp Stars*
Sharon Bryan

No. 120 *Cool Auditor*
Ray Gonzalez

No. 121 *Long Lens: New and Selected Poems*
Peter Makuck

No. 122 *Chaos Is the New Calm*
Wyn Cooper

No. 123 *Diwata*
Barbara Jane Reyes

No. 124 *Burning of the Three Fires*
Jeanne Marie Beaumont

No. 125 *Sasha Sings the Laundry on the Line*
Sean Thomas Dougherty

No. 126 *Your Father on the Train of Ghosts*
G.C. Waldrep and John Gallaher

No. 127 *Ennui Prophet*
Christopher Kennedy

No. 128 *Transfer*
Naomi Shihab Nye

No. 129 *Gospel Night*
Michael Waters

No. 130 *The Hands of Strangers: Poems from the Nursing Home*
Janice N. Harrington

No. 131 *Kingdom Animalia*
Aracelis Girmay

No. 132 *True Faith*
Ira Sadoff

No. 133 *The Reindeer Camps and Other Poems*
Barton Sutter

No. 134 *The Collected Poems of Lucille Clifton: 1965–2010*

No. 135 *To Keep Love Blurry*
Craig Morgan Teicher

No. 136 *Theophobia*
Bruce Beasley

No. 137 *Refuge*
Adrie Kusserow

No. 138 *The Book of Goodbyes*
Jillian Weise

No. 139 *Birth Marks*
Jim Daniels

No. 140 *No Need of Sympathy*
Fleda Brown

No. 141 *There's a Box in the Garage You Can Beat with a Stick*
Michael Teig

No. 142 *The Keys to the Jail*
Keetje Kuipers

No. 143 *All You Ask for Is Longing: New and Selected Poems 1994–2014*
Sean Thomas Dougherty

No. 144 *Copia*
Erika Meitner

No. 145 *The Chair: Prose Poems*
Richard Garcia

No. 146 *In a Landscape*
John Gallaher

No. 147 *Fanny Says*
Nickole Brown

No. 148 *Why God Is a Woman*
Nin Andrews

No. 149 *Testament*
G.C. Waldrep

No. 150 *I'm No Longer Troubled by the Extravagance*
Rick Bursky

No. 151 *Antidote for Night*
Marsha de la O

No. 152 *Beautiful Wall*
Ray Gonzalez

No. 153 *the black maria*
Aracelis Girmay

No. 154 *Celestial Joyride*
Michael Waters

No. 155 *Whereso*
Karen Volkman

No. 156 *The Day's Last Light Reddens the Leaves of the Copper Beech*
Stephen Dobyns

No. 157 *The End of Pink*
Kathryn Nuernberger

No. 158 *Mandatory Evacuation*
Peter Makuck

No. 159 *Primitive: The Art and Life of Horace H. Pippin*
Janice N. Harrington

No. 160 *The Trembling Answers*
Craig Morgan Teicher

No. 161 *Bye-Bye Land*
Christian Barter

No. 162 *Sky Country*
Christine Kitano

No. 163 *All Soul Parts Returned*
Bruce Beasley

No. 164 *The Smoke of Horses*
Charles Rafferty

No. 165 *The Second O of Sorrow*
Sean Thomas Dougherty

No. 166 *Holy Moly Carry Me*
Erika Meitner

No. 167 *Clues from the Animal Kingdom*
Christopher Kennedy

No. 168 *Dresses from the Old Country*
Laura Read

No. 169 *In Country*
Hugh Martin

No. 170 *The Tiny Journalist*
Naomi Shihab Nye

No. 171 *All Its Charms*
Keetje Kuipers

No. 172 *Night Angler*
Geffrey Davis

No. 173 *The Human Half*
Deborah Brown

No. 174 *Cyborg Detective*
Jillian Weise

No. 175 *On the Shores of Welcome Home*
Bruce Weigl

No. 176 *Rue*
Kathryn Nuernberger

No. 177 *Let's Become a Ghost Story*
Rick Bursky

No. 178 *Year of the Dog*
Deborah Paredez

No. 179 *Brand New Spacesuit*
John Gallaher

No. 180 *How to Carry Water: Selected Poems of Lucille Clifton*
Edited, with an Introduction by Aracelis Girmay

No. 181 *Caw*
Michael Waters

No. 182 *Letters to a Young Brown Girl*
Barbara Jane Reyes

No. 183 *Mother Country*
Elana Bell

No. 184 *Welcome to Sonnetville, New Jersey*
Craig Morgan Teicher

No. 185 *I Am Not Trying to Hide My Hungers from the World*
Kendra DeColo

No. 186 *The Naomi Letters*
Rachel Mennies

No. 187 *Tenderness*
Derrick Austin

No. 188 *Ceive*
B.K. Fischer

No. 189 *Diamonds*
Camille Guthrie

No. 190 *A Cluster of Noisy Planets*
Charles Rafferty

No. 191 *Useful Junk*
Erika Meitner

No. 192 *Field Notes from the Flood Zone*
Heather Sellers

No. 193 *A Season in Hell with Rimbaud*
Dustin Pearson

No. 194 *Your Emergency Contact Has Experienced an Emergency*
Chen Chen

No. 195 *A Tinderbox in Three Acts*
Cynthia Dewi Oka

No. 196 *Little Mr. Prose Poem: Selected Poems of Russell Edson*
Edited by Craig Morgan Teicher

No. 197 *The Dug-Up Gun Museum*
Matt Donovan

No. 198 *Four in Hand*
Alicia Mountain

No. 199 *Buffalo Girl*
Jessica Q. Stark

No. 200 *Nomenclatures of Invisibility*
Mahtem Shiferraw

No. 201 *Flare, Corona*
Jeannine Hall Gailey

No. 202 *Death Prefers the Minor Keys*
Sean Thomas Dougherty

No. 203 *Desire Museum*
Danielle Deulen

No. 204 *Transitory*
Subhaga Crystal Bacon

No. 205 *Every Hard Sweetness*
Sheila Carter-Jones

No. 206 *Blue on a Blue Palette*
Lynne Thompson

No. 207 *One Wild Word Away*
Geffrey Davis

No. 208 *The Strange God Who Makes Us*
Christopher Kennedy

No. 209 *Our Splendid Failure to Do the Impossible*
Rebecca Lindenberg

No. 210 *Yard Show*
Janice N. Harrington

No. 211 *The Last Song of the World*
Joseph Fasano

No. 212 *Lonely Women Make Good Lovers*
Keetje Kuipers

No. 213 *jump the gun*
Jennie Malboeuf

No. 214 *Apostle of Desire*
Bruce Weigl

No. 215 *GREEN OF ALL HEADS*
Aracelis Girmay

No. 216 *Pluck*
Adam Hughes

No. 217 *Disaster Tourism*
Rena J. Mosteirin

No. 218 *The Appendectomy Grin*
Charles Rafferty

No. 219 *The Serious World*
Laura Read

No. 220 *At the Gate: Uncollected Poems 1987–2010*
Lucille Clifton
Edited by Kazim Ali

No. 221 *August, September, October*
Craig Morgan Teicher

No. 222 *This Elegance*
Derrick Austin

No. 223 *Sidekick*
Naomi Shihab Nye

No. 224 *I Am Trying to Love the Whole World*
Jenny Browne

No. 225 *Pagan Sky: New and Selected Poems 2000-2025*
Michael Waters

COLOPHON

Boa Editions, a nonprofit publisher of poetry and other literary works, fosters readership and appreciation of contemporary literature. By identifying, cultivating, and publishing both new and established poets and selecting authors of unique literary talent, Boa bring high-quality literature to the public.

Support for this effort comes from the sale of its publications, grant funding, and private donations.

The publication of this book is made possible, in part, by the special support of the following individuals:

Anonymous (x2)

Angela Bonazinga & Catherine Lewis

Caccamise Foundation

Peter Conners

Bonnie Garner

Albert Goldbarth

Alison Granucci

Janice N. Harrington & Robert Parker

Peg Heminway

Sandi Henshel, *In memory of Anthony Piccione; In honor of Anthony Piccione's daughters*

Chuck Hertrick & Joan Gerrity

Kathleen Holcombe

Nora A. Jones

Kitty & Nick Jospe

Christopher Kennedy, *In memory of Michael Burkard*

Joe & Dale Klein

Michael Martone & Theresa Pappas

Joe McElveney

Daniel M. Meyers, *In honor of J. Shepard Skiff*

Boo Poulin, *In memory of A. Poulin, Jr.*

Deborah Ronnen

William Waddell & Linda Rubel

"RAISE YOUR VOICE"
CAPITAL CAMPAIGN SUPPORTERS

In honor of Boa's 50th anniversary, the following individuals made significant contributions to our "Raise Your Voice" Capital Campaign. We are grateful for their generous support.

To learn how to join the chorus and raise your voice to ensure another 50 years of independent publishing visit: www.boaeditions.org.

Anonymous

Kathleen Holcombe

Joe & Dale Klein

William Waddell & Linda Rubel